SCHOOL OF UDHRA

NATHANIEL MACKEY

CITY LIGHTS BOOKS
San Francisco

Cover design by John Miller/ Big Fish Books
Author photo © Paul Schraub
Typography by Harvest Graphics

Library of Congress Cataloging-in-Publication Data

Mackey, Nathaniel. 1947–
    School of Udhra / by Nathaniel Mackey.
      p.   cm.
    ISBN 0-87286-278-X : $9.95
    I. Title.
    PS3563.A3166S36 1993
    811'.54 — dc20   93-21774
                                                                CIP

City Lights Books are available to bookstores through our primary
distributor: Subterranean Company, P. O. Box 160, 265 S. 5th St.,
Monroe, OR 97456. Tel: (541)-847-5274. Toll-free orders (800)-274-7826.
Fax: (541)-847-6018. Our books are also available through library
jobbers and regional distributors. For personal orders and catalogs,
please write to City Lights Books, 261 Columbus Avenue, San
Francisco, CA 94133, or visit us on the World Wide Web at:
www.citylights.com.

CITY LIGHTS BOOKS are edited by Lawrence Ferlinghetti and Nancy
J. Peters and published at the City Lights Bookstore, 261 Columbus
Avenue, San Francisco, CA 94133.

Some of these poems first appeared in the following publications: *ACTS, Avec, Bombay Gin, Callaloo, Conjunctions, Epoch, Hambone, Ironwood, lower limit speech, Mandorla, New American Writing, Notus, Quarry West, screens and tasted parallels, Socialist Review, Temblor, Tyuonyi, ZYZZYVA*.

CONTENTS

I. SONG OF THE ANDOUMBOULOU: 8-15

Song of the Andoumboulou: 8	3
Song of the Andoumboulou: 9	4
Song of the Andoumboulou: 10	5
"Blinded. . ."	6
Song of the Andoumboulou: 11	7
Song of the Andoumboulou: 12	9
Song of the Andoumboulou: 13	11
Song of the Andoumboulou: 14	12
Song of the Andoumboulou: 15	15
"Day one stood erect, arthritic. Ache. . ."	17
"Day two's bright bed of attraction. Unsnuffed. . ."	18
"Day three fell away in fragments. . . ."	19
"Day six. Lidless eater of raw meat, day. . ."	20

II. OUTLANTISH

Melin	23
Irritable Mystic	25
"Nut's belly bloated with stars. . ."	28
Knotted Highness	29
Degree Four	32
Sweet Mystic Beast	34
Amma Seru's Hammer's Heated Fall	38
"Abstract. . ."	41
"Sweet. . ."	42
Alphabet of Ahtt	43
"To've been there as they. . ."	45
"Spent. . ."	46
"Synchronous flavor. Mendicant. . ."	47
"Awoke stranded on the island of. . ."	48
Out Island	49
"Thinking then. . ."	53

III. ZAR

Wizard of Ought	57
"Thought of his brother. . ."	62
"Each thing its due the ostensible. . ."	63
Tonu Soy	64
"Far spot of warmth we remembered. . . ."	69
"Where the would-be City squeezes blood. . ."	70

Aspic Surmise 71
"So incensed. . ." 72
"Theirs though there we. . ." 75
"They the receding we we might've. . ." 78
Far Over 79
"Blue loop it turned out. . ." 83
"Gave Ttha. . ." 84
"Then during our descent. . ." 85
Slipped Quadrant 86

for Pascale

I

SONG OF THE ANDOUMBOULOU

8 - 15

First to be born were the Yeban, small creatures with big heads, discolored bodies, and frail limbs who, for shame of their condition, hide in the holes of the earth. They coupled and gave birth to the Andoumboulou, who are even smaller than they are. All these beings were born single. All were incestuous because, like Ogo his progenitor, a Yeban male coupled with his daughter, an Andoumboulou woman. Thus, the earth's interior became slowly populated with these beings who are the very first to attest to Ogo's failure and his lost twinness.

— Marcel Griaule and Germaine
Dieterlen, *The Pale Fox*

*Visita
Interiora
Terrae;
Rectificando
Invenies
Occultum
Lapidum.*
— Alchemy

SONG OF THE ANDOUMBOULOU: 8

— maitresse erzulie —

One hand on her hip, one hand
    arranging her hair,
                blue heaven's
bride. Her beaded hat she hangs
from a nail on the danceroom
             wall. . .

    As though an angel sought
  me out in my sleep or I sat up
    sleepless, eyes like rocks,
             night
like so many such nights I've known.
  Not yet asleep I'm no longer
    awake,   lie awaiting what
stalks the unanswered air,
             still
    awaiting what blunts the running
              flood
or what carries, all Our Mistress's
         whispers,
            thrust
    of a crosscut saw. . .

    Who sits at her feet fills his
    head with wings, oils his
           mouth
    with rum, readies her way
    with perfume. . .
        From whatever glimpse
 of her I get I take heart, I hear them
          say,
  By whatever bit of her I touch
I take
  hold

Took the dust of an eroded footprint,
    rolled as if thru dirt I'd
    see the coming forth of suns.
      Sowed ruins of what by then would
whose walls collapse and
                  crumble,
     dervished air so thin one's
               heartbeats
                    hum. . .

Uplifted arms of an Osirian ropewalk,
               erratic
    moonsluice, Legba's crutch.
           The
  unswung dancers of Thoth, wide-eyed
             interpreters,
    their book the loosed embers
             of dusk.

New bud of musk immersed in
    limitless cloth, moored
abundance of clouds collecting
          pools our
   palms cupped.   Our palms keep,
     their muddied waters near
    the root of the world-axis
          tug
    our boat's, our bed of sweat's
              blown seeds. . .

The body floats. The oldtime people sing,
    say hurt is light angels eat,
    come whispering meekly by the
             banks
of the beautiful river,
       Bread of ash, bed of
            caiman's
         teeth

Sat up reading drafts
of a dead friend's poem, papers
kept in a book I hadn't cracked
in years. . .
Rugs burnt Persian red repeated,
echoed, red ink like an omen of
blood.   Red ink as if to be
echoed at knife-point, ominous
tongues
inadvertently touch. . .
Burnt
red, the night white inside, painted
cave on whose floor her feet,
splintered, go numb. . .

Legs ascending
some unlit stairway, saw myself
escorted thru a gate of
unrest. The bed my boat, her look
lowers me
down, I rise from sleep,
my waking puts
a wreath around the sun.
Puts blood
back inside the sun, paints a face
on whose lips my lips, blistered,
ignite.
Taut legs. Long. Lengthening shadow. Deep
inside one stumbles. Rugs burnt. Burning.
No light.

Baited lip. Love's lawless
jaw. Said, "I love you,"   loaded
like
a pointed gun.   Burnt rugs needed
only a spark, spoken, ember.
Spilled ink. Prophet's red.   Struck
dumb

   Blinded

     by what likeness I saw. Exotic Persian red
       robe I put on this morning. Mad at the
world and at the mention of loss a new convert

                             to light. . .

     And at the mention of light a new convert
      to what at whose coming on even breath

                          gave out. . .
      Shook as though caught between warring
      darknesses, torn, blinded by what

                    likeness

  I saw

SONG OF THE ANDOUMBOULOU: 11

— school of udhra —

I sit up holding you a
year ago, yearning, let
   go, draw short of eternity,
    allergic to time. . .

To be found after waiting
so long but found wanting. . .
   Toward the end I saw mint
                   leaves
     bloom, bamboo blossom, saw
the soul off to its alternate
                 light.

Acidic juice of a just picked
orange. Acidic sweetness of a
   trumpeter's kiss. A jug of
    wine, a bag of asafetida,
   full-to-bursting calabash,
               bowl
turned upside
     down.
    All to say the end had come around yet
   again this time for real, planet long
     since about to blow away every
    minute now, clusterbomb canister,
    innocent fist of a child. . .

Ins and outs on the brink of a
   mending always under assault,
  love allergic to time, mourning
              love's
   retreat but with a backward glance,
an over-the-shoulder look says we're no
          longer needed.

An ominous cloudbank woke me with
  a kiss, belief thicker than
blood but empty. . .   Blackness
   lighter than breath,
            insides
of a blow turned inside out. . .

As if the air extracted an itch
  dug deep in the blood, earth's

fitful ruler,   rightful collapse,

                            lines
drawn against givens,   abject
    address by what would not
be done

Weathered raft I saw myself
adrift on.

    Battered wood I dreamt I
drummed on, driven.

Scissored rose, newly braided
  light, slack hoped-for rope
    groped at, unraveled.
                       Braided star
we no longer saw but remembered,
  threads overlapping the rim
of a sunken world, rocks we
  no longer saw by extinguished,
Namoratunga's long-tethered
                     light.

    Breathing smoke left by the gods'
  exit. Scorched earth looked at
with outside eyes, burnt leaf's
                Osanyin,
    raffia straw beneath
  coatings of camwood
           paste. . .

Saw myself bled, belatedly
  cut, inverted blade
  atop Eshu's head,
            sawtooth
cloth of an egungun,
  thunder whet the edge
          of a knife.

    And what love had to do with it
    stuttered, bit its tongue.
    Bided our time, said only wait,
            we'd see.

    Tossed-off covers.   King Sunny Adé's
wet brow.   Four twenties on the dresser
  by the bed. . .

    Cramped egg we might work our
  way out of,   caress reaching in
    to the bones underneath.

                                    Not even
        looking. Even so, see
                        thru.

        Watery light we tried in vain
            to pull away from.   Painted
                                        face,
            disembodied voice. Dramas we
                wooed, invited in but got
    scared of.   Song so black it
                                    burnt
        my lip. . .   Tore my throat as I
            walked up Real Street. Raw beginner,
                                                green
                attempt to sing the blues. . .

    Tilted sky, turned earth. Bent wheel, burnt
                                            we.
            Bound I. Insubordinate
                            us

Heart and tongue. These two meats, they are the right meat, they are the important meat, and they are the bad meat.

— Alhaji Ibrahim Abdulai

SONG OF THE ANDOUMBOULOU: 13

Bottom lip against my teeth

like a rock but unsteady,
                              stutters,
        "Fa. . ."

as in fox, as in Fon, as in fate.
        Raffia skirt, straw hat, raw youth,
    shimmering leaflight.
                              Shook
    me, made me shed my
                              skin.

    Coarse "cloth" like Legba
                              wore,
    rough skirt.
                Scratched air,
            inarticulate
                    lipsmear. . .
    Lizardheaded cane. Human
                              headed
        snake.

        Threadless tether, shadowed
    early morning eyes, moist
        hair, no pillow. . .

                              Riven lip
            sucked, almost bitten,
                              given back.

    Bones thought broken,
            mended,
                    reassemble.

        Endless night now
                    ended,
        rebegun

11

SONG OF THE ANDOUMBOULOU: 14

— uninhabited angel —

Again what speaks of speaking.

Boxed in but at its edge alludes
    to movement, loses us,
  flight.

      Finds its voice between bleeding
lips bitten into, the pointlessness
of going on.

    Under its breath between promises
mutters, "Would it were so,"
             bedouin
glimpse of what once I reach after it
    vanishes.   Fox's feet.   Zigzag slip.

  Fell asleep underwater it felt like. . .

    Phantom ledge, faint bodiless drop. . .

Drawn up, dredged archipelago.
                A capella
                      grunt,
    pebbles under the tongue. . .

              Again we
    began to move. Breathing rock,
              receding
wall.
      Wandering stone, something whispered
in my ear, lost course. . .
          Bent voice, an
    evaporative kiss, wet quivering
  lip. Quick bit of emptiness, bedouin
    window I peeped in thru,
              rope
unraveling turned me, torn,
        unstrung. . .

  Knew what once we'd have thought would
be the last of it wasn't. Spells we cast,
             caught
  up in. Vacuous bauble tossed about
by wind. . . Reached in with fishbone

fingers,
combed out the underwater woman's hair.
Thread of nothingness, needle of light I
laid hands on.   Lidless.   Lip
split,
stitched. . .

Infectious wind strung with
leper's bells, shrill sermon. Twisted
neck, net bursting with light.
Ominous
mouthful, taste of its ripeness. . .
Bested by warnings, arrived
wasted,
turned back. . .

Looked into as
the last eye closes, furtively
lit by what we already knew.
Without remedy, up all night two
nights
before, strict motionless engine,
sugared
sweat, wet hair my pillow, spoken
of as if spoken for. . .
That we'd each
know an alternate ending, move to speak,
mouth
wired shut. . .
Mute lure, blind mystic
light,
lost aura.   Erased itself,
stuttered,   wouldn't say
what

•

Sat up sleepless in the Long Night Lounge, love
stood me up. Stayed away though its
doing so stirred me. Wine on my shirtsleeve,
wind on my neck.

Nodded out, all
hell broke loose, blind earth, blue heaven.
Burst of adrenaline. Dreamt I was dreaming, drugged,
boated
back and forth between ruts.
Reign of

13

sameness, flat magicless world said I'd
eventually see it.   Cost me myself,
wooed me.   Wouldn't say when.

Saw by light so abrupt I stuttered.
                                    Tenuous
            angel I took it for. Took it
        for lips, an incendiary kiss,
            momentary madonna. Took it for
                                    bread,
condolences, cure. . .
                        Arrested in flight
            as though we throve on obstruction.
                                    Crook
                of an angel's arm, rickety
                crutch. . .

                        Sense of an entrance.
        Torn between closenesses.   Adamant
                rock worn down to dust. . .
                                    Desert
        song I sang throughout it all soothed
                me, said I'd already seen it.
                                    Fooled me.
            Wouldn't
                say what

14

SONG OF THE ANDOUMBOULOU: 15

— bedouin wind —

Back down the steps I go out
careful not to cross my legs
turning left up Monmouth,
     pressing
my feet to an otherwise all
      but
unbearable stretch as to a lizard's back.
  In the scorched upper lefthand
heavens my sister sits weeping,
 robed in kerosene light.
     Our father's
gone Panamanian grin's pathetic air,
thru which its teeth now push their deeprooting
 rotted stumps, unruly gunmetal
     gristings,
      a Dogon
  ram's head with Amon's gourd stuck
between its horns. . .

    Outside the
windowless room I dance a
clubfoot's waltz, my legs driven by horsemen,
  bones hounded by lusts.
     The last of
eight to pierce the lighted way, my
path readied by drumrolls, the
oils of Amentet, the raw throats of
      devotion. . .
Lipless thirst, our thumbless layings
 on of hands. . .

    The rough body
of love at last gifted with
     wings, at
last bounded on all but one
impenetrable side by the promise
 of heartbeats heard on high,
     wrought
promise of lips one dreamt of aimlessly
     kissing,
 throated rift. . . Furthered hiss of its
     gift
 of tongues. . .

So this my Day, my Light's
numberless years' run of horses
whose hoofs plow any dreamer's
head, my Day of bone, my bootless
feet
mashing shattered glass, at last
begins,
white stucco walls reflect a stark summer
sun.

A distant hum the faroff buzzings of
bees, boats towed ashore. . .
The noise recedes thru every usable
gate. . .
Unruly goat, so uncorruptly
unswung,
legs rusted. . .

The risen woo the wind and
are blown
away

Day one stood erect, arthritic. Ache
of its arrival, peregrine spark.

Seated each on a bedouin throne, sun
blown in our faces.   Blistered
                                    kisses.
Desert love.   Threaded
                        lips

Day two's bright bed of attraction. Unsnuffed
   ember, amniotic floor.   Blunt

  sustenance, mired sublime, remote,
    whispering, lost cry calling,
                  no way out
  if not thru.   But stuck, too
beautiful. "Stay."   Blunt sustenance.
    Sifting the choked water
                for bones. . .

  Seated each before a sea of exhaustion,
  off to one side of us prompting us,
    lipped indelicate teachers,
              heart's meat
raw, rough taskmaster muscle,
             carnivorous.
                  Cannibal,
   careless law

Day three fell away in fragments.
    Unfinished fourth. . .   Unbeginnable fifth. . .

    Wanting it back but glad one
gave it away, to've let go holding
    each breath as if it was
    or would be one's last.

    Warmed-over gospel. Stick-figure truth.
Sang with a cricket caught inside my
                  throat.

    Stuck tongue I sucked singing thru
cracks in a falling wall. Maybe my
    own, maybe someone else's.
               Stuck
    tongue bloated, foolish beauty.
            One's own

Day six. Lidless eater of raw meat, day
scoured by starlight,   breach
of it blessed but if only by music
by nothing,
house made of thrown-away stones. . .

Cast off
only to be called back,
cut,
sewn up again. Tenuous
throatsong, hoof to the head waking
up, plucking music from a meatless
rib. . .

Rickety tauntsong. Plum's pit.
Staining the hands with henna.
Close to the heart but keeps
out of reach,
Digitaria. . .   Home.   Bedouin
stone's
throw away

20

II

OUTLANTISH

"mu" fourth part -"mu" eleventh part

. . . a myth is not merely a word spoken; it is a re-utterance or pre-utterance, it is a focus of emotion. . . . Possibly the first *muthos* was simply the interjectional utterance *mu.* . .

— Jane Harrison, *Themis*

. . . a continent of feeling beyond our feeling. . .

— Robert Duncan, "Apprehensions"

MELIN

— "mu" fourth part —

Close by but
so remote,
drawn off
   to this or that ungraspable
   "it."

   Spoke of loss,
   relatedness, lack,
                  eligibility. . .
      Never another time
   like the first but
      to be free of its
                  memory.
This they'd pick their
      hearts out aiming
                  for.

   Abstract embrace but
      absolved of its
      imprint, fleshtone
                  taken
   up an octave,
               aired.

   "Eating meat cooked
on a crocodile's eye"
                  their
   name for hunger.
                  Meaning
   light. Meaning weight of a
                  ribcage
      cut up in dream after
      dream of thin men.

      The inevitable Two
         known as tender but
         sore, sated "sleeper"
            crouched among
                  rocks
      overlooking the sand at
                  Mosquito Bay.
   Recalling that year the world
      was only her slender
      feet, her seductive

23

leghair. . .
Saw that what light
there was came in
thru a two-way cut, blood
pointed elsewhere,
out,
"it" the intuited pass
they clamored
for.

Serenaded
by words they'd erase the
sense of, hearing its
whisper,
wind-afflicted hymn.

Adamant
flute amid muted brass,
baited
light. Dailiness, weight of a
life preserved in salt.
Lost as
they began to reminisce,
fleeting foothold. . .

Heard it again.
Cupped.
Hollow.
Hummed

IRRITABLE MYSTIC

— "mu" fifth part —

His they their
we, their he
  his was but if
need be one,
          self-
  extinguishing
I, neither sham nor
  excuse yet an
alibi, exited,
       out,
           else
  the only where
he'd be.

      Before
the long since
  remaindered
body, imagines
each crack, each
  crevice as it sweats
under cloth,
        numbed
inarticulate
       tongues touching
down on love's endlessly
warmed-over thigh.
          The awaited one
  she mistook him for haunts
  him, tells him in
  dreams he told
       him so.
  Such offense,
but at what
  won't say,
       moot
remonstrance,
      no resolve if not
  not to be caught
       out. . .

Abstract advance, its
advantage unproved,
  unbelieved-in,
       vain

what wish would
give. . .
                Late eighties
                            night
momentarily bleached by
        bomblight. Awoke,
    maybe inwardly wanted
                            it,
        wrestling with dreams
                            of the
awaited one again.
                        Thought
back but a moment later
        what moodier start
    to have gotten off
                            to,
    angered by that but
begrudged it its impact
                            and
        so sits remembering,
        pretending, shrugs it
off. . .

            Arced harp. Dark
        bent-over body. Esoteric
        sun whose boat its
                            back
    upheld. . .
                    Unseizably
vast underbelly of
                        light,
        limb-letting thrust.
                        Tread of
        hoofs. Weighted udders of
dust. . .
                His it their she
once they awake,
                            the
        arisen one,
                        world
        at her feet,
                        her feet
        one with their
                        rapture,
    ankledeep in damage
                            though she
        dances. . .

                        26

The slippings off
                    of her
of their hands define
her hips, whose are
    the suns whose
                    heat
        his nights taste
                    of
and as at last he
    lies her legs loom,
                    naked,
loose gown pulled from
    her, sleep
                turns.
And he with his
                postures
    cramps the air,
                bent
    lotuslike, lips
            part kiss,
                    part
        pout

Nut's belly bloated with stars
corrupt with gods. Beneath
        our year's new growth of
                                eyelids
            unlit eyes kept running
        come strumming the starlight,
                                stroke
        night's watery
    locks

KNOTTED HIGHNESS

Thin of limb, thick
   spread of hair
   whose locks that night
   he lay tied up in.
Close-to-the-bone.
   Prescient. Passing
               thru
  set against its wait.
Wafted scent said yes
   without saying it
                 outright,
   never to be numb to its
                    allure. . .
   Felt fragrances bore
  them aloft, phantom
   lift. The day of their
   descent a day closer,
commiserative wings
   extend a would-be
               embrace,
  feathered wish, thin
   would-be breath she
  took.

         Carved heart.
  Thin bent-over body.
   Arced harp cut from
             wood
  one night brought up
what's under.
        Masks
  made of trembling.
           Paint.
  Purgatorial stealth.
          Made of
its amends an unappeasable
             indulgence.
  Makes of them its
        then,
  of it their
      if.

      And as
if her hand had been

                    a five-stringed harp
                                    he
        hears it now,
                            hair
            smelling gently of
            headsweat, lipstick,
                                steep
                inextinguishable
                                kiss.
        Begs its glow never go
            away but even so
        to be rid of remembering,
                "rescue," the rare
                bird of Bandiagara's
                                    bentlegged
            sway before falling
                                down. . .

            Awaits word of the ark's
                descent, roused
                hammer. Hit by what
        he hears or thinks he
                                heard
                as if by both. The way it
                                    might've
                been yet less unlikely might've
        not,   that a stone sprouted
                    wings by spreading
                                        which it
            broke its fall

                            •

        And of B'Fox's beansifter ark,
                that a bentlegged insect
            bit it.   Bruised fruit,
                alveolus bean,   forked
                                        speech,
            spread beside a salt lake
                pink with flamingo
                                    feathers.
            Word of this crept inside
        their heads "and began
                                to spin,"

            by which they'd have meant
        that form despairs of content,
                rescinded what before

                            30

                                    they'd have
          thought prophetic. . .

                               Watching
          memory's masquerade, misnamed it
            Nommo's honeycolored hat.
            Fractious height braided
              swirls fell down from
                                    jaggedly.
            Foxfooted, zigzag drift.

          Clipped wing, thinskinned
            extremity. Clenched extremity,
          nub of what was.
                               Roughwinged
            angel, love's heated flutter,
                                         made
              an incense of
          intimate sweat

                          •

            Battered roof above their
          heads.   Beaten earth underneath
                their feet.   Bent
              legs they tiptoed in
                               on.
            Stirring up of stubs,
                               blunt
          would-be wings.
                          Not the eye but
            some other organ. A scent,
                               synaesthetic,
            led them on.
                          Not that looking
          ruined its allure but they
                               wondered
              what would it be like without it. . .

            Against the wall they wrote
            outraged on, a bough bent
              by wind with no voice inside it.
          "Swayed as we sang," they
                               sigh,
              thinking, "Would it were so,"
                                         rocked
              but not by it,
          unwon

                          31

DEGREE FOUR

There though where they
were regardless,
elsewhere. Mat made of
  tossed-off straw.

Tissuepaper
house worn atop the
head. Tissuepaper
    boat, lit up
                inside. . .
  Vanishing thread,
bleached burlap
            sack. . .
    Took one step
  forward, took
                two steps. . .

Took to being taken
past the breaking
  point, muttered
            legless,
    "Hard light, be our
    witness," wondering why
      were they no match
                for
drift.   Saw that this
was what history was, that
    thing they'd heard of.
Ferried across Midnight
    Creek on a caiman's
                back. . .
  Saw themselves made
    to eat uncooked rice. . .

Kept in a room called
Búsinêngè Kámba, put
to work.   Saw this too
  was what history was.
                Desolate
  seedpod,   mother-in-law's
      tongue,   tongued rattle.
  Footless romp, reflected
      light on flooded
ground. . .

32

              Rolled a
joint with gunpowder
  inside, struck a match,
whispered, "This is
   what history does."
  Said, "Above sits
     atop its Below, each
  undoing the other
even though they
                    embrace."

  Went up in smoke, lit
by feathers of light,
   debris falling for
                    ages. . .
This as they thought,
   what was known as
   history, this the
                    loaded
gun carried under their
                    coats. . .

   "Wooed by fish under
   shallow water. . ."
                    This
too their sense of
   what history
                    was.
Fleeting glimpse of
   what, reached for,
                    faded,
   fickle sense of what,
   read with small sticks,
                    caved
in

"That ugly voice is not my brother's. Go away!"

Again the *Zim* went away disappointed. He knew that it was still the voice that betrayed him, and now he made up his mind to seek advice and have his voice doctored. He went to see his fellows at some other part of the forest. When he told them his problem, one of them said, "That's very easy. If you want your voice to be thin and smooth and sweet like a boy's, take an axe and roast it in a very hot fire. When the axe itself becomes red hot, take it out of the fire and swallow it. After that your voice will deceive the people in the rock."

— A. C. Jordan, *Tales from Southern Africa*

SWEET MYSTIC BEAST

for Johnny Dyani, Abdullah Ibrahim,
Joe Malinga, Dudu Pukwana. . .

Gruff
stutter,
scuffed horn.
Awoke weeping.

Lips dark. Bendable
bronze. Torn
fruit. Blubbery
sun, sucked,
                    inebriate. . .
Slept.

Rock's
ah, no such
answering. Numbness.
Mudjadji's
weighted bath, dated
                    "when". . .

Collapsed lung,
inexhaustible
snare. Squat
city.
        Walls,
pinched
voices, paper
        thin

34

·

Hunk of metal
strapped around
the neck. Not
a horn if not
          bellowing,
     heavenly bull
     broken loose,
               cracked
     egg with "eight"
          rhythms inside.

Southern hunger.
Brotherly voice.
               Blunt
     runaway hoofbeat,
          hollowed-out
earth underfoot.
                    False
     bottom, risen up
     from, winded,
                    blown
     back. Altered earth,
          beneath fox feet,
flew. . .

          Bellowing beast
     become squawking
          bird. Announces
     new meat for the
                         coming
     slaughter.
               Swift wing
too elusive to touch,
     acoustic wind-assisted
     wing which took us
                         in,
                              takes us
     under

·

Slivers pass between us.

Where we touch blue flutes
     pursue us. Hollow
     sticks bitten into,

blown.
Blue splintered wood
gotten under the
skin. . .
Blue noose made up of
cloth, billowed curtain.
Wind which might've
roped us, ravenous,
clawed
air clenched, unraveling,
raw. . .

Stone cloak. Newly dug-up
star. Broken-into
crypt of King So-and-So's
father.
Potted plant, painted skin
held up on a stick,
predynastic potmarks. . .
Fated
blow by then a sculptor's
touch, twisted feather,
animal air the heated
axe
made sing. . .

Flubbed note.
Unfunny valentine.
Forthright
warmth by metal made
suspect, secretive. Lied
about, looked at
crookedly,
caustic. Parrot's egg.
Promises.
Plucked.

Torqued wonder. Scripted
hit. Honeybird wing
turned into a
turban. . .
Cannibal air the axe,
heated up, swallowed,
made sweet.
"Maphundu
the Nodulated
One". . .

Sings only an abducted
"we," an aborted
      history, hurt it
   rehearses dancing
      the dance of a
                  knock-kneed
crane. . .
         Crabbed air,
      clawed way they
         had with it,
                  having it
      made but for made-up
sorrow,
         What's-His-Name's
      grudge against this or
that sibling run amok,

                        beast
      caught in the bell of a
                  horn

AMMA SERU'S HAMMER'S HEATED FALL

for Ed Love

Stood with lips pried
apart. Metal monster,
                            iron
thigh. Meskha made of
    lapis, lit chrome.
    A sideways look,
                        word
let out edgewise.
                    Iridescent
    wing, the Ancestress's
    vault's inverted
    bend. Arc lifted up
    out of limbo,
                    spat-on
shoe one could see one's
                        face in,
        bitter what light, what
        labored light it let
                    shine. . .

Shut mine, bent shepherd's
rod. Underground wail with
                            chrome
    conductor.   Crashed
    car, dents beaten out,
                        all
    bumper. Brash alchemical
    armor, philosophic polish,
        lapis-lit chrome.
                        I sing of
shine, the machine wrecked,
    resurrected, banged-out
    Osirian story told in chrome,
                            tone
    a metallic taste out of
tongue's reach, tauntsong's
    eternity, "Taht."

                    Momentary
    tent made while moved away
                            from.
Rotating face at the entropic window,
    stain spread inward, epistrophic
    thaw. . .

38

Dread love, knotted
highness
one would squint looking up to.
Levitated. Lifted. Locked.
No
life but what looking askance
let in, eyes momentarily exed,
corrected, atavistic two-headed
beast,
one head we call Stride, the
other Obstruct. . .

Blue light, so
bright it blinded. Rubbed it
away but at a loss for looking
saw nothing. Close, the ostensible
abode of the arisen. Bitten
we'd have been had it been
a snake.
I sing of shine, say
be my breastplate, harmolodic
horn hung round the neck my
hauberk,
hawk's beak, Horus's Eye.
Second
sight, second why. Why
seconded, squared. Coils
round an iron core, one
spot come back to again and again. . .
I sing of shine, the dead
dying of thirst come back
in chrome, voice bittersweet
though boyish, blood runs,
tauntsong's
eternity, "Taht."

Turned
head, inadvertent angle. Something
said to have been said, lips
welded, sparks flew. . .
There,
though if other than for reflection
none would say, wondering,
coming forth, where they'd come
from, edgewise informant, small
axe,
tall tree. . .
Shut mine, buffed would-be

39

breastplate.   Harmolodic armor,
   lapis-lit chrome.   Crashed

                       car,
  dents beaten out, all bumper. . .
Wrapped round an open cut, same

                          sore
   come back to again
and again

                              Abstract
        embrace but at arm's length
                                  intimate.
        Two rows of teeth weaving cloth
        we can't cut.
                      A dozen dots encircling
   a thirteenth born of blood,
                          star
        weaned of light. Born of paint,
        penitential debris. Clavicular
                              spillage. . .
            Valvular cut. . .
                        Bred of law but
        absolved in such myth as the Nommo
                                      catfish's
            growth of teeth. . . Torn body tossed
        out into space, head weighted with
                                      worry
                and of pinched aspirations
        knowing all.
                        Perked ears picking the
                                          air. Stray
   melody. Memory's
                      arithmetic
        straw. . .
                  On this to've elbowed in
        beyond remedy,   adroit band of
                                    wind
            men breathing together
                              that a
          crow's caw warn
                        of its
                              coming
        down

                                        Sweet
         beast whose horns mourn lost
             amenities, mystic lament it
                                        appropriates,
             mad but won't say. Sings out of the
         side of its mouth.

             Between sips from a
                 glass of rum, second
                 sight. Growled as we
                                        began to
         ignite, reassemble. . . Propped
                                        on what were
                 said to've once been legs,
                                        got up
         and walked

ALPHABET OF AHTT

for Cecil Taylor

Anagrammic scramble. Scourge
  of sound. Under its brunt
   plugged ears unload. . .
                       Tight squeeze
toward a sweatless heaven.
     Anagrammatic tath. Anagrammatic
   that. . .

       Shucked husk. Severed
  rope tossed upward. Not
    knowing why but reaching
                        elsewhere,
   edgy. Not without hope though
   how were we to take it as
   they yelled out, "Nathtess's melismatic
                          ttah"?
Not knowing why, we looked straight
  ahead, shrugged our shoulders,
  popped out fingers, we could dig it,
                    "What's next?"

     No muddier way to have begun we
    knew, none of us knowing whose voice
it really was we spoke with.
                  Something
  caught between the nose and throat,
                   buzzing
straw. Feathered wind outside its
   waiting place. . .
               A skittish reed
  whispering into one ear said,
             "By and by,"
we would understand it someday,
   someday move to make it happen,
                 twist
untwisted, roundaboutness put aside.

                 Tautologic
  drift in which once more what spoke
  of speaking spoke of speaking.
Made us wonder would it ever do
  differently, all but undone to've
   been so insisted on,
            anagrammatic

ythm, anagrammatic myth. . .

                                              Autistic.

Spat a bitter truth. Maybe misled but
       if so so be it. Palimpsestic

                                        stagger,

anagrammatic

           scat

To've been there as they
began to gather. All the tribes
of Outlandish crowding the outskirts
of Ttha.
As if to what wind had blown
them in to've answered any. Gust after
gust with no end in sight. . .
An intake
of breath by which birth might be proposed
of something said to've been known
as meaning made with a mouth filled
with air. The soul sucked in by something
said

as thru a crack in the door though the
doors dissolve. No way out if not in
was the assumption, austerity the proof,
strained

air, strung sea. . .
Thus that if when they
arrive we pretend we're asleep they
kick the doors in. Thus the unwitting
we

they ferret out

                                        Spent
        wish. An extravagant throb lately
    fallen from the sky, rapt Udhrite
                            espousal. . .

        Ache of its they the inundated earth
        we lament, as ours rises up, upended,
                                    islanded,
        Ahtt unsounded,
    sunk

Synchronous flavor.   Mendicant
fill.   Frustration.   One
     with its rising, two
                    with its
going down. Ahttlessness's
                    inverse hoist. . .

          As of its plunge a pretender's
          kingdom,   otherwise
             not to be had, held on to
                         intangibly,
          known as it
          splits apart

Awoke stranded on the island of
Ahtt, light's last resort.
An aroused wind feathering the
whip
of its arrival, the world a rumored
snake's
tooth away

It may be that the world which our authors here describe in symbol-
ic language as the "eighth climate" will be seen by Western people
as the "lost continent." . . . They tell us that while the world with
extension perceptible to the senses includes *seven* climates . . . ,
another world exists, which forms the *eighth* climate. The ancient
Sages were alluding to this world when they declared that besides
the sensory world there is another world with shape and dimensions
also extending in space. . .

— Henri Corbin, *Spiritual Body and Celestial Earth*

OUT ISLAND

— "mu" eleventh part —

As we arrive the ground
again goes under. An
   empty dish pointed
up at the sky.

Recalls the "elsewhere"
  we imagined, dreamt
about years back,
           throwing
  snow at one another
one night when we
              were twenty. . .
  Foolish whim,
         wet
remnant where they
  "lived without
         dreams,"
  of whom we'd also
heard they "ate no
         living
thing"

      •

Adamite sun. Stark, too bright
cavedoor. Rollaway boulder,
  boarded-up sky.

Broken latch.   Better no
door than to be locked
out, lets others in.

              Longtoed women dance
        a Cat Island two-step,
           talk with a lizard
                            wears a
        red bowtie.

           Drunken start, drowned
        Atlantean root, repeated
           whisper.   Namesake,
                                undersea
           rift rearisen. Blocked,
              butchered brother. *Baja*
                            mar.

        Spanish heart. Rough
              watery cut. Numbed
        infibulated sister
              sipping pigeon
                       broth. . .

           Flatted A. Long ah re-
              peating after itself.

                            Ba. . .
           Broken body. Bartered
        parts

                          •

           As though the man we saw
        shot were me.

           As if "as though"
        were no protection, bullet
           real, one of many repeats.
              Never a life like
        the ones we heard about,
                                bucket
              of ash tossed out of a
        cloud. . .

        Bed of ash, white blanket
        of light,   parrot feather.
           Scattered script near the
              foot of the centerpost.

           Whatever "someone" we
        awaited long since lost,

                                    given
up on.   Giver of leafwater
         taken from the heads
    of the dead. Trickling
                              sense
    of having been here
                         before.

         Got a glimpse but
    before I could grab it
         went away.   Found for
    an instant, lost, let
                   go.
                         Fleet
         momentary fit. . .
         Again goes under, gotten
    wrong, says what. Says
                            better
    unsaid. Inside, bites back.
                               Spills
    rum, sloppily blows us
    a kiss

                      •

    Thin bridge beneath an inked-in
    sun, soaked earth. How soon
         what light we'd be the
    bringers of belied.

                      Moist
    air. Absent other we embrace,
         thin waist and thigh,
                            drink in
         whose body's hot rain, hear
    floods come. . .

    House like a sigh, sun's
    house a circle. Junkanoo
         headdress the other side's
                              cry.

    Found out as what began
    to reascend outlived
         its bouyancy,   bordered
         on lack, low fallow
         ground run away from,
                         fetish-

light, floundering,
        flung. . .

Forgives us our
botched observances.
             Bargain-happy
soul begs let it buy itself
    back.

      Called it fishflare,
troughlight, world at our
    doorstep, stood.
           Steadied
our gaze but, unready,
saw nothing, naked.
Austere, so unlike
            itself,
sunk

Thinking then
about what it meant, and
again, how not to anesthetize
desire, leapt into
figures,
called it "Calling it the
eighth."
Called it birth, bursting
open, out, sweet mythic smith's
redistributed viscera,
lit,
glow beyond Ogo's reach. . .
Calling it
wind inside a fonio seed, unruly
whir, house made of spinning
wood. Called it sketches etched in
snakeshit, yeast in the storied
house,
called it a brush made of cat-
fish whiskers, calling it
call-it-what-you-will,
bewitched. . .
Saw satisfaction on a bed of yeses
calling it eelpot. Steeped indignation.
Threat. Rhythmic imprint.
Wishful,
whispered, "Be my twin."
Calling it
raw, too crude a truth to admit.
Desperate.
Unrequited. Thicketed rush which
if we could we'd outrun. . .
Called it
caustic, luminous brew we sip
wincing, seed finally free of its
husk
albeit broken, world an erotic
inch
out of reach

III

ZAR

The *zar-tänqway*, or *qalicha*, will go into a trance and his *zar* will speak through his mouth, identifying the spirit responsible for the trouble and indicating the treatment to be followed, which may include the preparation of a scroll by a *dabtara*.

— Jacques Mercier, *Ethiopian Magic Scrolls*

. . . on the road
to the city of Zar
which is just this side of far.

— Larry Neal, "The City of Zar"

WIZARD OF OUGHT

i.

A threepronged
fork in the
    road. The
    first way, hit
by a car. The
      next, poison.
Third, he gets
           burned
   by a witch. . .

Whichever way, the
  same city left
behind, inside
         himself,
  he steps outside
  it, sets his clock,
          gets
   up to go see where it
is he'll have
      gone

ii.

Beset by some
wish to return,
   recaptures the
feel of her
  jutting lips'
        loose
  kiss,   lights
of the Eleven Light
  City, lights looking
like stars looked at
  from their perch
  overlooking Seville. . .
            Says
  of it as of its rise
   the resemblance
  lost, city long thought
to be heavenly,
        heavenly
gate waited
  at so

iii.

Said of
it it consumes
itself. Of time
only that it
would tell,
not
when, white river
spun round our
bewilderment,
revenant
mouth we'd
make our
own. . .

Long in love with
self-pursuit,
thinks had he
been in hell it
could've been no
worse. . .
Token of soul
such light as
he'd have died
to be
absorbed in, the road
unwinding like a
scroll,
were there no way he'd
have made one,
militant, ritual
fist
held high, pushed
on. . .
To've not been
earthless, othered,
ears perked addling
sense. Not to've
loaded
up, turned inward,
were
there the place he'd
have known it by
birthright we
thought,

watery thought so said
    to be womanly, marriageable
city, habitable
                her

        iv.

She'd wear the sun she
said.   He remembers.
  Had it been so he'd
    pretend to be a ghost,
                        have
      his way with her.
  Obliquely, baited
      by wings we can't
    see, part sex, part
  intangible drift. . .
                    What
shape there was he'd
  have sculpted, worked
  its rare "skin,"
                run
      from where the
  cracked wood's
                    warnings
  don't cease, lost ground,
                        low
Caesarean
            growth

        v.

City of spirit we lost
our way towards. Utopia
    lost in the mind an
  imagined musk.
                Lip
    she pressed her
                tongue
to. Tempted him.
                Thus
    to be dealt with.
            Waited.
                    "Soon
come"

Erlik, tsar of hell: "I will dive into the bottom of the sea like a duck
and I will bring you a pinch of earth in my beak." That is how the
earth began.

— Alar-Buriat creation myth

[— *"mu" twelfth part* —]

     Thought of Ayler's
two-toned goatee,
    noticed his
own had begun to
      gray. . .   Dim, dis-
    integrating door
she walked in thru,
             beginning
     even then to
     say goodbye. . .
            Thin
legs he lay wrapped
up in, lost body new light
   would be won by,
          dredged-up
    sunship,
         malleable
   star. . .

      Sweet crease
between cheek and
   leg, tight pantyless
rump his carved hand
         caresses,
curve of the earth had it
   been his to make.
        Dreamt
city he conflates with sex,
             sweat
   mated with mud brought
   up in a duck's beak, thus
to say there the new
         day
begins. . .
     Means by mud
some obsequious content,

                              strong
        sense having long been had,
        says it was there they
           were meant to be. . .

                              Thick
smoke amid Siberian laughter,
    as again it begins to
    unravel,   hoisted earth,
                              hissing
        logs' lament. . .
                        Ladderless
    rise to a suspect heaven,
        levellable stair never not
        to be insisted on, lateral
                              advance
what advance
                 there was

Thought of his brother
eleven years gone, the way
it all, no matter
what, gets away.
                        Blue
flute. Failed resolution.
Circular breathing no
match for disaster, reft
beyond capture, whirled
                        out of
reach. . .

And of his mother six
months gone, the way it all ever
after fell apart. Thinks of
death almost all the
time since then, the body
                        brought
him into the world wracked,
lungless, nothingness mapped, gone
into, only in dreams would they
be seen again. . .

                        Wakes up nights
wondering why,   the he they inhabited
shed like dead skin,   itching where
the light fell, scratched where
it would rise, the what-sayer come
from the east,   dilated
                        sky
run to riven
squint

Each thing its due the ostensible
end,   unmet. Mile after
   sometimes mile about which what
  more to say than that it
                   wasn't there. . .

   Much having been made of so
stripped a death, uneventfulness won
   for what cause it   made, intent on
                      spirit. . .
 Sweet-speaking userless drug the
  adamantine air,

  not to be made
a project of

TONU SOY

for Jay Wright

1

Though the namers
knot their tongues
ad infinitum.
      The
Gnaoua donning colors,
castanets, dancing,
  Bilal making
        Fatima
smile. . .
      Talk of
lungs and by
that they mean
  obstructed.
      Outmoded
language of spirit,
  emptied of content
he'd have believed
  had he not been
          theirs
to be instructed by. . .
          Plucked
gutstring, animal vestige.
Udhrite arousal. Udhrite
        address. . .
Made of wind, would-be
  world he wanted,
      aromatic
breeze as if lifting
her dress, part pubic musk,
        part
exotic perfume. . .

Skeletal escort. Boned
embrace. Bedouin wish
  to be elsewhere,
      every-
where at once. Swift,
  inextinguishable
rescue,   rickety witnesses
  though they'd
      be. . .
Fugitive kiss to

exact what purchase.
   Intimate qualm,
                infinitesimal
quiver. Quick twinge out
   of which a world grew,
                   moot
  world of which they grew
weary. Escorted in to the
Atet boat, belated orisons
                almed,
  ipsic, lest it
begin again

    2

  But again it
begins again.
  Book of sand, book
of salt, book of
    water. . .
           Relieved, it
  would say, of reference
    except to Martinho's
omnisicient
       sigh. . .
  Blue samba,
            sway,
swung sea-root.
  Ripe stomach the
  shape of an oud's back,
    bedouin drum
              struck,
  indigent sky. . .

And were the day of her
             descent
  to return, they hear him
say, an elixir he'd make of
  her necksweat, fetishist
              beads
  between fingers and thumb.
  Testamentary "teeth"
  wrapped around his
           wrist,
  thin etheric dress the eight
    limbs of their embrace, thin
    foxical spider's helical spin's
would-be rise. . .

Of which
the dreamt she cautions
ought not to, less in love
with him than with the moment's
accoutrements he broods,
                              bits
of light caught in the hairs
of his goatee. . .
                    By which
time they'd have arrived he
                              thought,
halves of a tale which had never
been told which when it was
would set them free he'd been
led to believe. . .
                    Something sung
in Spanish half-heard, half-
imagined, half-misunderstood
                              except
the words' recompense gave way
                                    to rhythm,
runaway wish not to be done with
wandering, Udhrite arrival,
                              Udhrite
dispatch. . .

                    Udhrite intent no sooner
there than abducted, Udhrite abscondity,
Udhrite repair. . . Book of
sun, book of salt, book of water. . .
Book of sand, book of waiting,
                              book
of been. . . By which to begin,
                                    ever
applicable, cystic, long since
arrived after so much flight
                              sick
of so much flight

3

A lark, they say, swallowed
the sky, sick of so much
flight. Fish wore suits of
sand, the singer watched
it all from a little boat. . .
                    Busted
gate now the rim of the world,

thetic doorway, world inextricably
in place, blue placenta,

$$\text{roots}$$

of the acacia tree. . . About
this they say only so much,

$$\text{lips}$$

hammered shut by some anomalous
light no such eyes as ours
would survive they say. . .

$$\text{And that}$$

the singer said, "Come with
me," and was refused, a
rose donned a suit of steel,

$$\text{sword}$$

and scabbard, gleamed as would a
god, a gazelle's eye they
say, stabbed and still bleeding,
book of thorns. . . Of this too

$$\text{they say}$$

only so much,   struck by some
enormous light no such eyes
as even theirs could endure

$$\text{they}$$

say. But that we, dressed in
black, revive them with salt
and by this they begin again. . .

$$\text{Book of}$$

sound, book of sand, book of
water. . . Book of glint, book
of glimmer, book of then. . .

$$\text{Thetic}$$

floor, falling foot rearisen, of
which the encumbrance at last
cleared away, seven shakes

$$\text{rousing}$$

wings fray the singer's
throat. . . Book of he, book of she,
book of him, book of her,

$$\textit{Them}$$

to the what-sayer's *Who is
this "they"?*, this their coded way
of continuing, that she came

$$\text{back}$$

but only briefly they say, as in a
dream, dressed as none of them
could recall, only that she
wore a scarf thin as a butterfly's

67

wings. . . Some loaded way
                                  this the
        way they repeated "sick of so
        much flight,"   spliffs
                              lit,
        chalices lifted, consequent
hum the what-sayer's *we*, whereof a
        new muse might emerge, root
                                  clarity,
        whimsic nearness, far-flung
                              sight. . .
        "Muy lejos," the chorus's refrain
        felt beyond hearing,   soulful
                                  she had
        said as they sat in the Ochún Café
eating moros y cristianos, meaning
        that mix, black beans and rice. . .
                                  Underneath
        something moved, ran away with him,
syncretist wish to be beyond schism,
        recollected bliss to erase the
        movement of troops, wall of
                                  money,
        rickety floor, boarded house known
        as history, ripped archetypal two
        told of in song after song. . .
Luminous wind Manuel sang about backed
        by overdubbed voice, guitar.
                                  Sweet
spit the insomniac sang about backed
        by flutes, unremitting drums. . .
                                  Without
        remedy, grunted, ground-zero, who
        had of late said yes, why not, so
        what, his part part fool, part
                              fox

Far spot of warmth we remembered.
    Scarified skin. Forest ash
       rubbed into cuts, flutes
       cut from wood brushed by
                     antelope
    horns, burnt   elephant
    tailhairs rubbed across
    bellies, chests, butts
               daubed
      in ritual spit meaning
                what?

    Ash around the eyes to aid
  sight, organs, bones and
     blood to come clothed anew. . .
    Hot quiet.   Ekimi mota.
                   Stolen
    molimo.   Uterine warmth. . .
  Moist rub, wet give of it,
            gift
    "fit for a king." Cleft whose
              regency
  pierced,   all as what world had spun
    our heads collapsed, breath beyond
    capture, wind out of reach. . .
               The escorted
     soul shown its way without
    drums, gourd rattles, less
  than as we thought it would be,
              deep
     dream's amenity
    gone awry

Where the would-be City squeezes blood
    from stone, stairstepped
  observance. Blunt
                    circumference
          met by movement, rhythmic
afflatus it can't contain. . .
                    Chaminuka sees men "with
          no knees,"   meaning white.
                              Fankía
      hears the guns of war.
                    Shot god, bitter
        book turned real. There they might
          look but that their gone gaze
                              grow there,
          taken,   meaning made at whose
      expense, twinned or twinless. . .
                    Twinless,
                              torn
  within

ASPIC SURMISE

1

Came dawn the pigeons
cooed Arabic under the
eaves outside their
    window.
              Winded prince
in bed with mannequin
    parts, lost elation,
   his the supplicant hand
                 at her
waist. . .
         Up late watching
election results the night
   before,   that year
the afflicted gave them
back their cures, wind blew
    kisses,   throat-clearing took
   the place of talk,
               rocks
ate their teeth. . .
          All the
way out where the river
spoke slang, the sun,
   trees, mud on their
             feet,
all blue. . .
       Left behind,
   we'd risen up,
           looked a
 curse into
 the ground

　　　　　　　　　So incensed
　　　we sang with our teeth
　　clenched, adamant music
　　　　　　　　　　the weapon
　　　of the weaponless, what
　　but wish to think otherwise. . .

　　　Tagged heads to be rolled off
assembly-lines next. . .
　　　　　　　　　Butchers
　　　in black tie, beast brought out in
　　　the beastly, "animals in human
　　　　　　　　　　　　skin". . .
　　　Against that this manyfooted,
　　musicfooted beast, basketmouth
　　　　begun to
　　leak again

Eked-out invective
to what avail. . .

Something some called history
traipsed in on fishfeet,
over the earth captivity
spread like a gas,
                    trapped
        gas,
            greed's government
to grief soon come. . .
                        Governing
        beast met head-on by its
better, fake brotherly
        voice found out, fed
        back to itself, "animals
in human skin". . .

                        Split stem.
        Split reptilian stem.
                        Revolution's
        axe "a cool breath on the
            back of the neck."
                        Said with
        such clipped inference we
heard it played on apinti
                        drums. . .
        Slick preachment.   Opiated
spin.
        Made amends with what spiritless
chill shook them at bed's edge,
        nothingness not unpossessed of
        an appeal,   in dreams to be
                            seen
        again. . .   There though resistant
to touch, looselimbed abscondity's
intuited imprint,   taken up as
                            weight
and in dreams undreamt: eaglebone
        piccolo, syncretistic feel,
        spurned access,   quiddity's
                            worded
        skirt's thin weave,   third wish
                            that
wishing cease. . .   Late wash of
        what passed for affection. Refused

resurfacing, hobbling in warptime.
Watery flute run. Hatchet-headed hawk. . .
False muse what might've been,
fugitive glimpse made myth years
later, silhouetted legs' bright
backdrop of sun. Gouged eyes

                                        given
back their gaze turned inward,

                                                limbs
taken up untouched. . .

                                Stared
lidless, caught by resemblances,
hemorrhaging sun so dispersed we
dreamt we bled incessantly,
blood pleading exile's

                                        end. . .
Though by that it begged its
own undoing,   atavistic
wheel turning into we

                                turned
into whir.

                        Rolled as if inside
some risen skin, rhythmic moult out
which a conch call carried

                                us
on

Theirs though there we
were, whereabouts not known, new
    ground undone.   Blue match
  blown out,   blue breath to the
                              kindling
      of marrow,   memory,   blood. . .

Bluelimbed leaper.   Feathered stretch.
   Dirty sock slipped under caesar's
door. . . Come at last in light of
                              impending
     collapse to speak of soul, shot
  splendor talked about so convincingly
                                  we
      winced,   chickens beat their
      wings as we walked in. . .

                              Raw skin, legs
     dusty with legdust,   tautologic drift,
                                  otherwise
     untouched. . .
                 Out on the balcony, the bazaar
         less than a stone's
     throw away,   algarabía
        buzzed,   bit me,   took
                          my
   tongue

                          75

3

To unmean with moaning,
adamant,
    guttural gist inexhaustibly
ancestral to itself. . .
    Bent glyph, synaesthetic,
unglimpsed. . .

Swift hit, abstract
arrival. Syllabic stretch,
    loose thread whose
arrival, come late,
                  comes
    as if not at all. . .

Endless clack chasing
    would-be reflex.
                  Collectivity-
wish meant to ward off
death.
      And with blood calling
    out to blood, though if
    by blood what was
meant missed its target
                what then?
Kiss taken at cliff's edge,
    homage and reproof,
solemnity's last resolve. . .

    The regime's death around the
    bend. Taken away with it. . .
Never again enough to have
    begun with qualms, begged
forgiveness, each that
all extremity return thru a
    central point,
                fierce, not
yet navigable demise. . .

                Gathered
    godless, they the remembered,
moaned might moaning do the
    work of guns. Under command of
whose hum heads turn,   psychic
    twitch,   sophic light's
                baited
    look turned intimate,

                                        irritant
wish to be more intimate still.
Gouged earth. Late glacial
    estate. Doorpeep's nod,
    near side of eternity.
                            Carolina
        rice washed ashore by shipwreck. . .
Stepped expectancy. Oxygenated
rush. . .

        Dredged elders of which
    we were each becoming one,
        numbed enough not to have
    noticed,   agitant clap
whose fluted echo
                    egged us on. . .
    Nothing there not made to matter,
    mischievous. Ripening towards
collapse.
        Scattered image
        brought abreast of itself,
        even so, an oblique tongue's
                                tally
unexpelled

      ————————————

    They the receding we we might've
been. This their collapsed
     expectancy,   fraught
soul so bone-close, teasingly
  discreet,   not to be made an
                      object of.
     Yet of this they made
       something else, wondering
     for what if not imagined
                impact.
  Root world whose arrested gleam
    they'd reignite. "Music,
               mend our
     hushed unwillingness," they whisper.
                       Dream

    dreamt in euphoric
    recoil

FAR OVER

Slit sky the pool
we approached. Of
that what lipped
                    amendment. . .
    Lit spliff. Burnt
spear. Split squint. . .
    Too intense a look
tantamount to a lunge.
    Upstart suzerainty.
    Ovoid embrace. . .
                    But to
        be done with it
once and for all,
                    flat
    fifth and all, thin
                    ragged
voice going on again
    about love. . .

                    Cracked
    shell. Heard hearts
        break, resonant,
        remote, Zar no farther
        off than a breath,
    putative hoofbeat,
                    breath
unassured even so.
                    Evanescent
    mesh, limb twined on
        limb. Sprung polity
from under, horsegod,
    hoofprint. "I-nity."
                    Tenuous
    kin. . . No him, no you,
                        no
    her, no them. Nipped,
non-pronominal ought
        we called Ouadada,
    I   and I   and I
        ad infinitum,
    more than we can say
    we saw. . . No bedouin
        stone the builder
                    refused,

no longer the one wailing
let it be the one.
Catquick, made mistakes
look like dancing,
irredentist gift,
                    irredentist
grudge. . .
                    New utopic
thought no sooner
there than discarded.
    Thin rope to walk, no
sooner there than
                    gone.
What other place
                    the words
allot we went after, no
    matter the what-sayer
                    said
so what. . .

                    Perched high,
told ourselves "I-nite" as
                    the way
    went on,   nudge nearing
loss of control, knocked out of
    heaven,   saw things, we
say, older than thought. . .
                    Of
the air itself, the far side
                    of sight.
Crossed Ethiopian eyes
                    ignite. . .
South we see Rast, west we say
                    Tsar,
    north fraught with whether,
with what-say, what we thought
    lost, late bloom of magnolia,
come so far not knowing
                    for
what

Inasmuch as we leapt it
lay beyond us, sandrofia
    the song said catch. . .
                Thrown
  ghost, resistant wind
    insistent we listen
    to the reed's complaint.
      Tent of wonder. Ouardia's
  gown. Silhouetted legs
the lineaments of light,
    refracted, reached
                for
though they withdrew. . .

                 Illusory
  pool. Peripatetic lure,
            prosthetic. . .
Shook if so much as brushed by a
    hair. . . Arced encounter,
              covered
  we were and by that
touched "I-ness" to "I-ness,"
    inward, wombed inducement
    arced into "us-ness,"
      otherness, nothingness,
               Nephthys,
    Nut. . .   Inductees
    into the academy of N'ahtt,
    taken lately to mumbling
          sitting
  alone on stoops late at
        night,
    lost hand we held holding
          our own. . .
  Irredentist wish, meeting the
    dead in dreams. Dressed
    as if nothing had happened, except
  they wear shades getting out from
    the backseats of cars,
         bones
too stiff to embrace.
         Irredentist
myth, "mu" meaning lost ground,
         "else"
  the earlier where we were
      after. . .

Never there. Never not. . .
No release

Blue loop it turned out
we were caught in.
Came to among those
who say last meaning
latest. Sledged
we might as
well have been.

Blue lump love cut its
teeth on. Soul
set wandering,
susto. . .
Andalusian fishbone caught
in our throats coughed up,
cante
moro, Mauritanian
strick. . .

Adamant rope where the world
receded. . .
Ahttlessness kept us
afloat. . .
From there we
saw glittering sea, blue loot,
strung gem plucked oudlike,
poignant,
what would all
again and again
fall away. . .

Not so not unlike need,
inexact.
Not to be redeemed or
remedied,   midnight
tears, torn cloth, same
as ever, never
the same

                              Gave Ttha
               to those gone before,
                                          the way it all without
                    fail fell apart. . .
                                    Sack of
                    woe,   sack of eaten
                    earth. . .   Requisite
                                              silence.
                    Requisite stone. . .

                                    Demanded
                of us a lament we bled
                                    words
                    to, guns went off in our heads. Heard them
                say run, they'd be there waiting for
                                              us,
                    come

                             Then during our descent
down Ahtt-Nut Hill. . .
                             "Sink or
swim," we heard. "Sullen
                                    swing. . ."
Though they swam we sank,
    called it swamp.

                            Regarding which,
           knowing what we knew,   who'd have not
           wanted out? Spin within a
                             spin,
                     eaten away at.
              Had it been other than
                they'd expected,
                           who'd
    have known?

                          Bandaged head. Mute
        book we read from, the
           imagined we never
                       to rest
     where they
           were, would it would
                      cease

As if by late light shaped of its
arrival,   echoed announcement
        come from afar,   loosed
        allure,   the as-if of it its
        least appeasable part.
                                        Rich
        tense within we called it,
            would without end,   seed
    within a seed sown elsewhere,
                                        somewhere
        said to've been known as
Ttha.
                Wrought   surfaces, putative
    soul,   cheated heart.   Shot
        body borne up to be looked
    at, learned from, one
                            heretical
moment's reprimand. . .
                            Something a
        Sufi said in Andalusia.
                            Something
        said to've been said before.
    Ominous music made a mumblers
                                    academy,
            vatic scat,   to be alive
    was to be warned it said. . .

                                    And of
        loss long assured of its
            occurrence,   echoed
        agreement grown more remote,
                                    long out of
            reach,   not as yet known by
            name though not nameless,
                                    swift,
        uninterpretable design. . .
                                In oblique
        league with majesty,   secret,
    unannounced,   came to where the
        flutes of the Afar spat salt,
                                    limbs
    under loosefitting cloth. . .
        Came then to within a stone's
        throw of Ttha,   very far,
            weary, felt we'd walked with

on our feet.
Saw the in we sought
ran on, some said stop, some
we'd barely started.
Stood us
up within sight of Ttha, strewn
kin, sat us down sipping hog's-hoof
tea. . .

Trashed ecstasy. Impudent if.
Said
what but wind on our stomachs fed
it, whim. Felt for it falling away
from it, called it "Calling it the
earth,"
unsprung.   Shied away might worry
cease, drew near, bud bursting out
out of earshot, wind out of India,
three-digit heat.   Scratched
air
screamed reparation, strung spillages
fingers pried apart as they
struck. . .
Running start without which no escape, with-
out Rasta's far-eye squint   not
see. . .

Numbed comfort.   Lungless bellower.
Believed it.   Faith gotten back,
as if not,
broke in on its answer, made its caught
mouth twitch. . .   Grew numb,   having
nothing to say, said so.   Glum,
though if need be not.   Encephalic
blow.
Hollow emblem.   Blocked.
Heads wet,
many a midnight soaking. Slogan-weary
sleepers. Dream of a just world.
Saw the in we sought ran deep, sat us
down with chills, polyrhythmic
shivers. . .
Pinched earth, outrun by longing.
Whimsical inlet.   Renegade
wish

Photo by Paul Schraub